Blue Peter

D1138957

Book 33

Written by
Anne Dixon,
Steve Hocking and
Richard Marson

9

10

11

12

15

14

3

THIS BLUE PETER BOOK BELONGS TO

....

....

....

3

Contents

Hello

Welcome to the thirty-third Blue Peter Book. It's packed with all the most exciting things that we've done on the show since Book Thirty-Two was published. So much has happened since then, and we hope that you'll find some of your favourite moments here. You can take to the skies for a world record and a leap of faith. You can join us in a bobsleigh for a run down the track, or in the saddle for a horses' holiday. You can travel the world with the team from Memphis to Marrakesh, and from the gondolas of Venice to the war canoes of the Solomon Islands. Closer to home, find out how Blue Peter is put together in the studio when Simon becomes the first presenter to direct the show.

Another first, and a proud moment for all of us, was when Matt won the BAFTA (British Academy for Film and Television Arts Award) for Best Presenter. Liz weighed in with her bronze medal in the British Bobsleigh Championships. For one day only, Konnie swapped jobs to become a live weather forecaster!

It's been a great year for dressing up, too. Just check out the four of us

There!

looking the part for our special James Bond programme. And we dressed up to play the detectives in our mystery serial The Quest, too – see pages 21, 26 and 45 for a Quest adventure exclusive to this book.

And this was the year we were helped out by a foxy new member of the team, CBBC superstar Basil Brush, who became a firm favourite with all the pop stars appearing in the show.

2003 was the fortieth anniversary of the launch of the Blue Peter badge. To celebrate this milestone in our history, we've launched a special limited edition of this famous and highly prized possession. You could win one by sending us an idea for the show. We'd love to hear from you. Lots of our best ideas for the programme come from our viewers. Keep telling us what you like to see on the show and, you never know, maybe one day you'll be in it yourself!

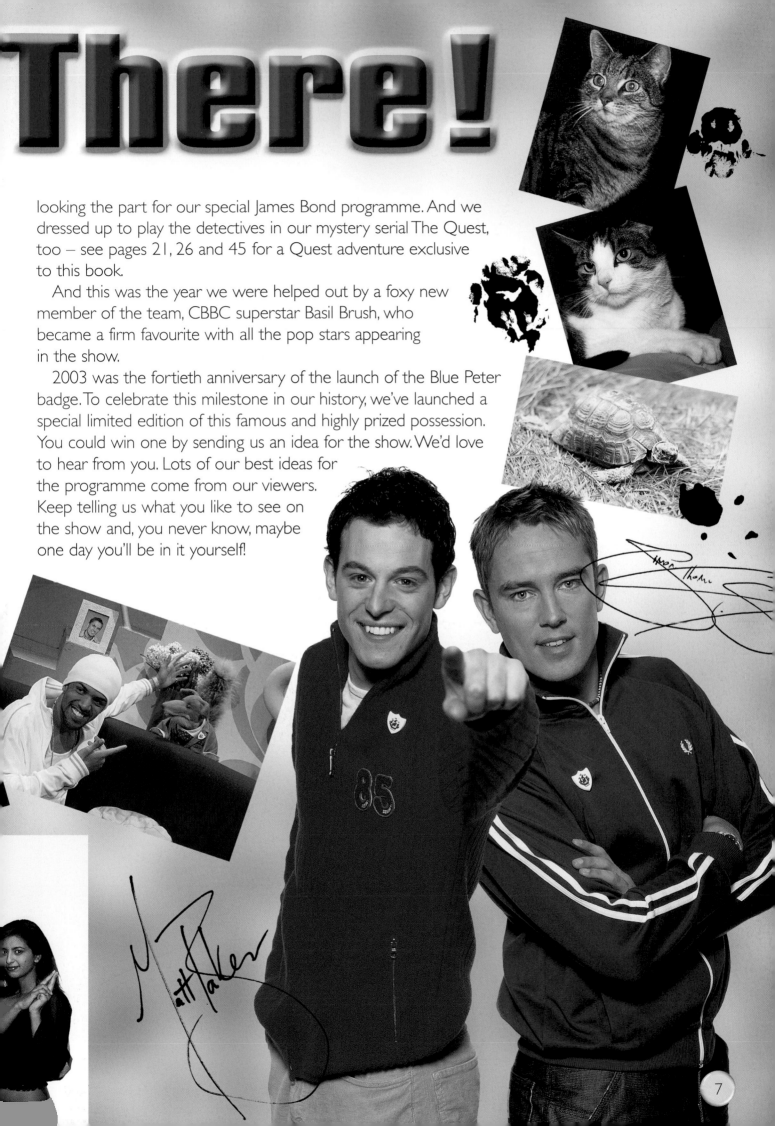

Postcards from Morocco

Morocco is two-thirds larger than the UK, but half as many people live there. One of the reasons for this is the huge area of sand in the south that forms part of the Sahara Desert. Morocco is a land of dramatic landscapes and beautiful colours.

We'll never forget our camel trek across the dunes towards the setting sun. Camels have always been valued because they are so well adapted for life in the desert. They can drink up to a quarter of their own bodyweight when they find water, and can manage without drinking for up to ten days. They store fat in their humps in case they don't find food, and their wide hooves are perfect for walking across sand.

For one of our programmes we looked at the colours of Morocco. Konnie got very close to the colour blue made from indigo. It was quite a handful!

Matt's brush with colour took him to the tannery at Fez. It's a shame we couldn't bring the smell back with us - it was awful!

The dyes for leather are mixed in huge clay vats, and Matt wore his wellies to get close to the action.

9

We've often flown kites and surfed on Blue Peter, but no one had tried both at the same time. Simon learnt to kite surf in Essaouira. It wasn't easy!

Neither was it easy learning to climb in the heat of the Moroccan summer. It took the best part of a day for Matt to complete his climb up the Todra Gorge. In the picture on the left, you can see our cameraman, Will, who had to climb, too!

This is Liz with the women of Tidziu in the south-west of the country. They run their own company producing oil from the nuts of the argan tree. The oil is made by crushing the nuts, and can be eaten and used on people's skin. The nuts are often pulled down from the trees by goats, who love the fruit!

We met some remarkable people in Morocco, but none more so than Ali Louche. Ali is a Berber nomad and lives in the Atlas Mountains with his family and their animals. They move their tent from time to time, so finding Ali was an adventure in itself. Ali and Matt got on really well, and agreed to keep in touch when Matt went home.

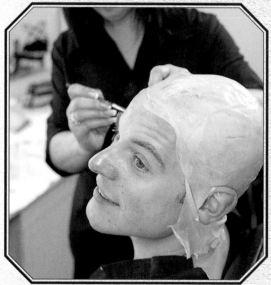

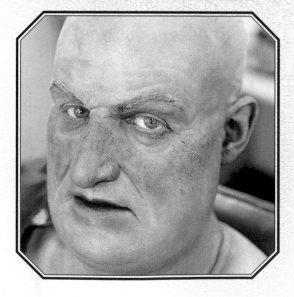

'Enery the

I t all started with a call from the Blue Peter office. "Matt, we've got the six wives of Henry VIII coming to the studio!"

"Haven't they been dead for a few hundred years?" I asked.

There was a sigh on the end of the line.

"Yes, well, these are the waxwork versions. And guess who's playing their husband?"

What I didn't realise was that this would mean much more than just dressing up. Movie make-up maestros, Aaron and Marilyn Sherman, who have worked with the likes of Robert de Niro and French and Saunders, had agreed to transform me into Henry VIII as he was at the age of fifty-two. This is about as different from how I look as it's possible to get.

It would take over five hours, so I reported to Make-up at the crack of dawn. Aaron and Marilyn had created three pieces of foam rubber, which were glued on to my face using a specially designed medical adhesive.

Then a base coat of make-up was sprayed over the mask to give an even skin tone, before Marilyn got busy with layer upon layer of grease paint to make the latex skin come alive.

It felt a bit like having a soft pillow pressed into my face – not too unpleasant, in fact. The hardest thing was having to sit still for so long, and I could only eat or drink through a straw, which meant soup for lunch.

Eighth, I am!

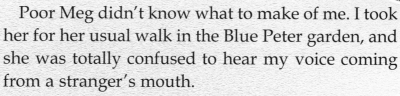

Poor Meg didn't know what to make of me. I took her for her usual walk in the Blue Peter garden, and she was totally confused to hear my voice coming from a stranger's mouth.

Aaron and Marilyn were still putting the finishing touches when that day's programme went 'live'. With my wig and beard in place, I just had time to struggle into my padded fat suit, which gave me the correct body shape, and put on my royal costume. Then I stepped in front of our studio cameras so that Konnie, Liz and several million viewers could give their verdict.

The girls were impressed but, like Meg, they preferred Matt to His Majesty. To show everyone it was still me under there, I removed everything, layer by layer. As our closing music began to fade up, I just had time to give one last command, "Off with the viewers!"

P.S. My day as Henry VIII gave those bright sparks in the Blue Peter office an idea. If you turn to page 48, you'll see what I mean!

BARKER'S BOB

Peter

25

ROYAL AIR FOR

Formula One on ice, the fastest thing on sharpened steel – it's bobsleigh, and I was going to ride that knife edge.

The 2003 British Bobsleigh Championships were taking place at the Austrian Olympic run in Igls, and I was joining top driver Michelle Coy as her brakeman. What was I thinking of? This was no place for beginners! Michelle had other ideas, and after intensive training at the British Centre of Excellence for Bobsleigh we were off to compete in the two-man race.

I wasn't sure who was braver, Michelle or me. I had experienced the speed of the bob as a passenger on a four-man sleigh, but if I was to help Michelle I had some serious preparation to do. It's necessary to keep walking the course until you know every turn by heart. We needed as many practice runs as possible, too, if we were to stand a chance in the Championships.

Our day of official training was exhausting but it was essential. I piled on extra layers of clothing and lots of padding in case of accidents, and wore special shoes with ice spikes.

Who were our main competitors? There were three other teams competing, and Michelle and I were definitely the outsiders.

Race day arrived. We watched the experienced competitors set the pace and I knew we'd have to give it everything. Michelle and I mentally prepared for the run, visualizing each bend of the course. Then we took our position at the start for our first timed run. Michelle shouted the command to go, and in less than one minute we had completed the course. As we crossed the finishing line I pulled hard on the brake handle, but it flicked out of my hands. We were heading towards the trees… Miraculously, I regained control of the handle and we stopped just in time. It was a scary moment, but then good news came over the tannoy, "Speed, 108kph. Time, 57.37 seconds."

Michelle and I got ready for our second attempt. My head was buzzing and I could feel the blood rushing around my body. Michelle shouted the command and we were off again, flying around the bends. We had done it! What was our position? Incredibly, we'd come third.

Who would have believed that Barker's Bob took Bronze in the 2003 British Bobsleigh Championships! What a proud moment, but I owe everything to Michelle, who was brave enough to take me on. Thanks, Michelle!

Sun-Dried Simon

During my time on Blue Peter, I've been lucky enough to visit Italy several times. My favourite place is the city on the water, Venice. It's probably the most photographed, written-about and talked-about city in the world.

There are no cars in Venice so, if you're not on the water, you're walking. I enjoyed strolling through St Mark's Square with its flocks of pigeons and elegant cafés. Napoleon called it "the drawing room of Europe", and it still is, today. Looming over the square is the Campanile, or bell tower. I was allowed to stand at the top early one morning as all the bells were rung. It was an ear-shattering experience!

I was also given the chance to test my skill and nerve on the water as a gondolier. The design of gondolas has stayed the same since 1562, and being a gondolier has often run in families for generations. Gondoliers wear a very distinctive uniform and, because tourists are willing to pay extremely high prices for a ride, they make a good living.

Carnival masks have been a trademark of the city for hundreds of years. Everywhere you walk, there are tiny shops crammed with countless examples, from the comic to the scary. Traditionally, masks are worn during carnival time in February, but they are made and sold throughout the year.

I had a go making a mask for myself, and although it took ages to finish, it was an incredibly satisfying thing to do.

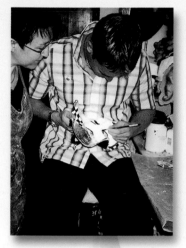

The heat from the furnaces was extraordinary, and the whole process seemed pretty dangerous to someone who didn't know what he was doing. The end result was a vase with a very thin neck, a perfect gift for my mum!

Sadly, Venice faces an uncertain future. The age of the buildings, pollution and global warming are all possible reasons why this fabulous and unique place could disappear under the sea. There are many ideas about how to prevent such a disaster, and we can only hope that one of them succeeds. For the world to lose such a truly magical place would be a tragedy.

I wasn't so sure about my attempt at another Venetian tradition, glass blowing on the island of Murano. I don't speak Italian and my teacher didn't speak English, but we muddled through somehow.

"Carrots, cabbages, apples and pears. Cheap as chips!"
Wherever you live, there's probably a market where stallholders shout out what's for sale, just like the soap-opera stars on EastEnders.

We created a mini version of Albert Square Market and it got a big thumbs-up from actor Todd Carty, whom you're bound to recognize as former EastEnders' stallholder Mark Fowler. Why not make a mini fruit and veg stall of your own?

You will need:

1 shoebox with lid
Ruler
Black pen
Scissors
Glue
2 empty matchboxes
4 lengths of dowelling or garden canes
1 aluminium foil box
Modelling clay in fruit and veg colours
Re-usable adhesive
Green felt or fabric
Green stripy cleaning cloth
Green card (for boxes)
Tissue paper (for inside boxes)
Brown paper
String
Paper clip
White card

Market Stall

1 Turn the shoebox upside down. Measure and mark 4cm from the long edge nearest to you on both short edges. Draw a line between the marks and carefully score along it. Cut both ends of the shoebox up to the marks. Bend the flap downwards along the score line and outwards to make a shelf.

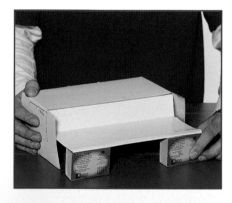

2 Glue the matchboxes lengthways under the corners of the shelf to support it. The shelf can be used to display goods.

3 For the canopy supports, use four lengths of dowelling or garden canes. You can make them any height you want, but 35cm is about right. Make two holes in the back corners of the box and two at the back of the shelf. Push the canes through until they are level with the bottom of the stall.

4 To make a shelf to prop up boxes of fruit and veg at the back of the stall, cut the aluminium foil box in half, diagonally across the ends and then lengthways. Cut the shelf to fit the length of the stall. You may need to trim the corners to fit around the canes. Use modelling clay or re-usable adhesive to hold the shelf in position.

5 Cover the whole stall with green felt or fabric. Make a few slits in the material so it fits snugly around the canopy supports.

6 To make the canopy, cover the shoebox lid with the stripy cleaning cloth. As a finishing touch, shape the edge so it looks like a real canopy. Place the lid on top of the supports, and you're ready to get on with the stock.

Roll yellow clay into a sweetcorn shape. Lay two flat strips of green clay in a cross, and gently fold them around the yellow sweetcorn. Make enough of each variety of fruit and vegetable to fill a box, and display them on your stall.

9 Cut out squares of brown paper to make tiny bags. Thread thin string through a corner of each one. Hang the bags from a hook made from a bent paper clip attached to one of the canopy supports.

10 Write your prices in black ink on small pieces of white card.

11 For a finishing touch, you could make weighing scales. Use a 2cm length of cardboard tube and an oval bottle top painted silver for the pan. Draw a triangle on white card. Make one side curved and cut it out. Draw on a dial with numbers and attach it to the tube.

You can have lots of fun making stalls that sell other things. The basic stall is the same, but you could use different coloured cleaning cloths for the canopies, and different coloured fabrics to display your goods.

7 For boxes to hold fruit and veg, use rectangles of green card. Draw a border all the way around, and fold in the sides. Cut through one fold on each corner, and carefully glue the box together. Make several in this way, and line the boxes with tissue paper.

8 Use modelling clay to make tiny fruit and veg. You could make a bunch of bananas out of yellow clay. Tomatoes are simply red balls. Use white clay for mushrooms, adding a ball of brown clay underneath and an even tinier ball of white in the centre. Make carrots out of orange clay, and press two green pieces of clay, in the shape of a cross, onto the thick ends.

THE QUEST I

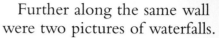

Chase Manor was a sprawling mansion with a high clock tower, surrounded by a thick, dark wood. Loveday, Jack and Will were there to solve a strange riddle. Their new client, Dr Ruddy, had been assistant to the famous scientist, Professor Chase, who had died suddenly. Before his death, the Professor had been working on a hush-hush project in his top-secret laboratory – so secret, no one knew how to find the entrance.

The only clue Professor Chase left to the whereabouts of the secret lab was "…pearls before swine may become pearls of wisdom…"
The plump and bustling Dr Ruddy was sure the entrance was in the hallway of Chase Manor, which was filled with a number of strange items.

A glass case was mounted on one wall. Inside it was *some kind of scarlet fish.*

By another wall was a stand. On it was a *skull which had all of its teeth missing apart from a few at the back.*

Further along the same wall were two pictures of waterfalls.
And by another wall was a plinth with a musical instrument on it.

"Did Professor Chase play the banjo?" asked Jack.
"It's not a banjo, it's a lyre," corrected Loveday. "But I'll wager he didn't. I think one of these items opens the secret entrance to the laboratory. I wonder if it's got something to do with pearls before swine being the pearls of wisdom?"

Jack thought for a moment. "It may very well do…*I think the pearls are keys and one of the objects in this room is the lock."*

"But which object?" asked Will.
"And how do we find the pearls?" asked Loveday.
Jack smiled. "Pearls before swine… pearls bee four swine!"

ELVIS THE

Soon after Henry VIII, Matt got to play another famous king – the King of Rock 'n' Roll, Elvis Aaron Presley. Although he died in 1977, his music is still as popular as ever. Elvis holds the UK record for the most number one singles scored by any artist in recording history.

The track Matt chose to sing was one of Elvis's early greats, *Jailhouse Rock* – hence the old-fashioned, American jailhouse costumes!

When Elvis started out, he quickly got the nickname, Elvis the Pelvis, because of his unique and highly energetic dancing. His hip wiggling so shocked parts of America that some television stations gave orders for him to be filmed only from the waist up.

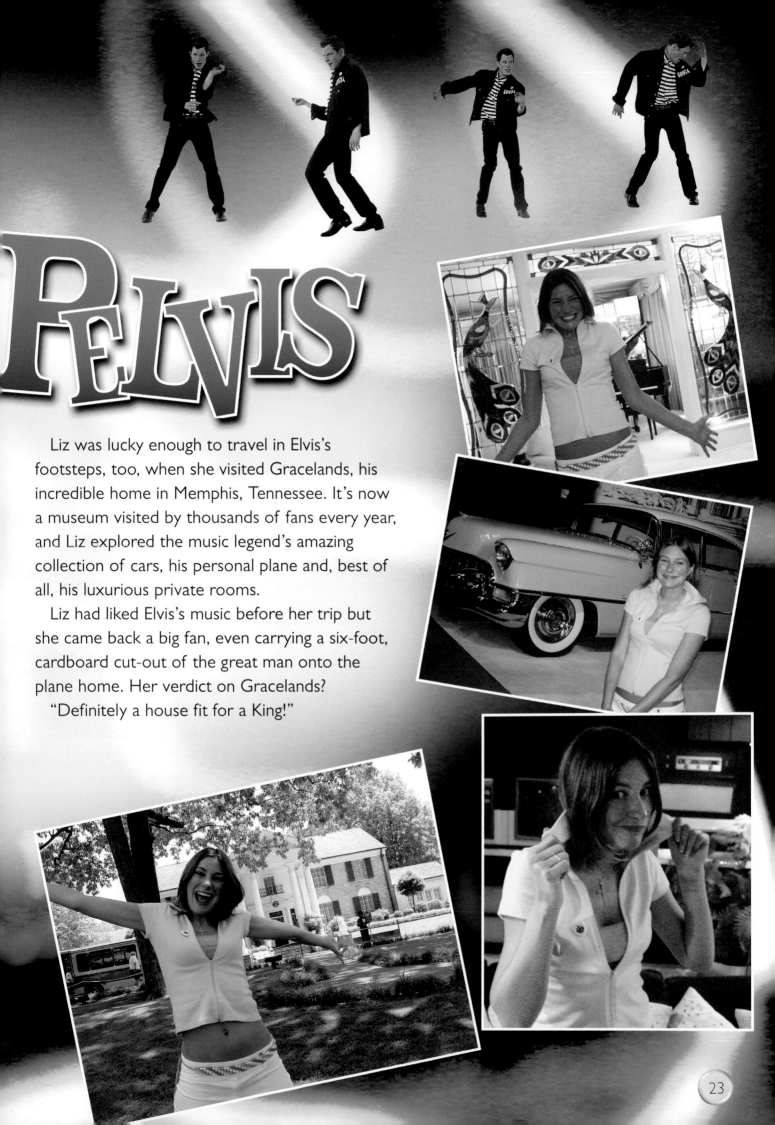

PELVIS

Liz was lucky enough to travel in Elvis's footsteps, too, when she visited Gracelands, his incredible home in Memphis, Tennessee. It's now a museum visited by thousands of fans every year, and Liz explored the music legend's amazing collection of cars, his personal plane and, best of all, his luxurious private rooms.

Liz had liked Elvis's music before her trip but she came back a big fan, even carrying a six-foot, cardboard cut-out of the great man onto the plane home. Her verdict on Gracelands?

"Definitely a house fit for a King!"

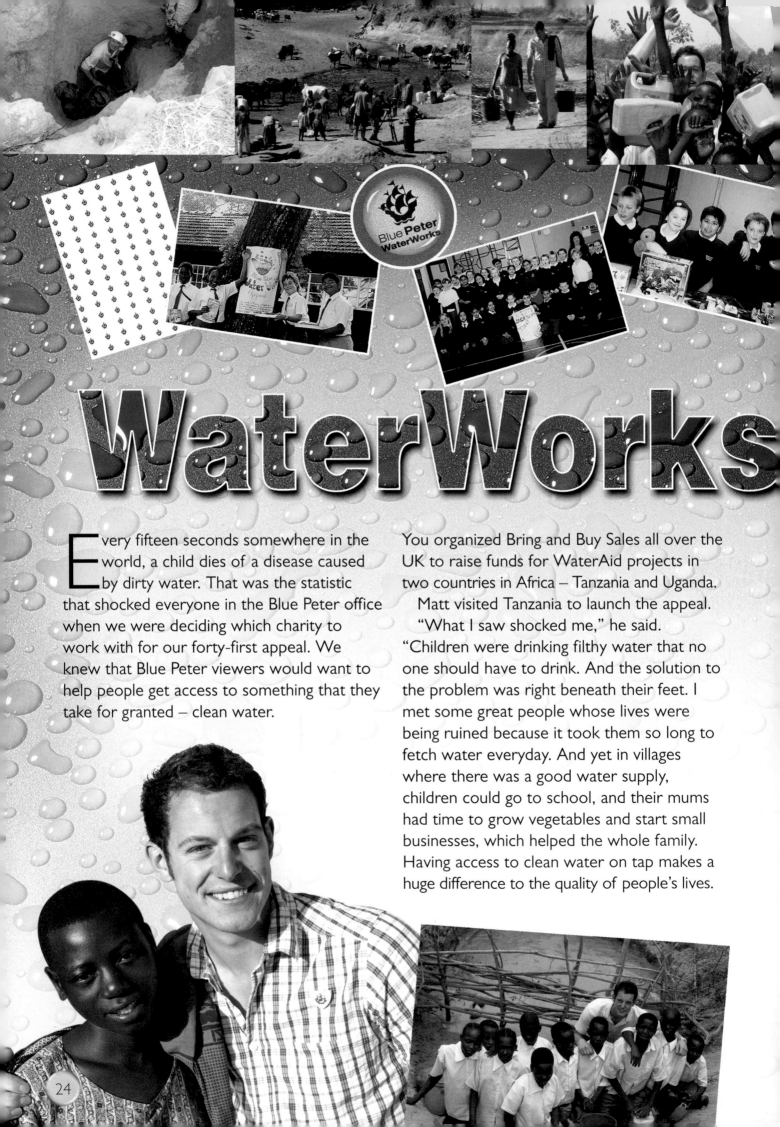

WaterWorks

Blue Peter WaterWorks

Every fifteen seconds somewhere in the world, a child dies of a disease caused by dirty water. That was the statistic that shocked everyone in the Blue Peter office when we were deciding which charity to work with for our forty-first appeal. We knew that Blue Peter viewers would want to help people get access to something that they take for granted – clean water.

You organized Bring and Buy Sales all over the UK to raise funds for WaterAid projects in two countries in Africa – Tanzania and Uganda.

Matt visited Tanzania to launch the appeal. "What I saw shocked me," he said. "Children were drinking filthy water that no one should have to drink. And the solution to the problem was right beneath their feet. I met some great people whose lives were being ruined because it took them so long to fetch water everyday. And yet in villages where there was a good water supply, children could go to school, and their mums had time to grow vegetables and start small businesses, which helped the whole family. Having access to clean water on tap makes a huge difference to the quality of people's lives.

Appeal

It was so simple and it made a real impression on me. I couldn't wait to get back to the Blue Peter studio and tell everyone about it!"

Thanks to the efforts of Blue Peter viewers, work started almost immediately in Nala, the village Matt had visited.

"There was no shortage of ideas for where to put taps. And no shortage of people to do the work," he told us. "The village leaders knew exactly what they wanted to do, and I'd seen in other villages how the local children could organize themselves into tap committees to keep the water supply clean. All that was missing was the money to buy the equipment to pump and pipe the water. You provided this.

It meant so much to everyone to have the equipment they needed. It was a project that wouldn't just last a few months. It would last everybody in Nala and the other villages we helped a whole lifetime. I was very proud to be a part of it, and if you ran a Bring and Buy Sale, or went to one, you should feel proud too!"

P.S. By March we'd doubled our target and smashed the £1,000,000 stage.

THE QUEST II

Staring through the gauze of a bee-keeping hat, Jack delicately reached into the hive of Peruvian killer bees. There had just been a hat and a pair of gloves, so his body was only protected by his normal clothes. He definitely didn't want to disturb the deadly bees.

He could see something white glinting in the honeycomb – he pulled it out. It was the pearl! But clinging to it was a bee. The queen bee. Enraged by the removal of their queen, angry bees began to swarm from the hive, looking for someone to sting…

Loveday clung to the clock face on the tower high above Chase Hall. She had guessed correctly that the pearl had been hidden in the number four, but while she was retrieving the pearl, the hatchway leading to the clock tower shut behind her. Now she was trapped on the clock face. She looked down – the ground was dizzyingly far beneath her…

Will was deep in the forest surrounding Chase Hall. He'd been looking for swine, but Professor Chase hadn't kept pigs. That would have been too easy. He'd found a swine, a huge boar, snorting and squealing. It had glistening black eyes, a thick hairy hide and sharp tusks as long as Will's arm. And around its neck was a locket with the pearl in it. Without warning the boar charged, trying to impale Will on its sharp tusks…

HANG GLIDING RECORD BREAKER

etting a world record isn't easy. Just ask Matt! It took two and a half years of planning, and many days of filming and waiting for the right weather before Matt and his pilot, Judy Leden, were able to tackle the world dual hang gliding altitude record.

Matt's first flights had been in the summer of 2000. However, a year of delays caused by restricted access to the countryside due to the foot and mouth crisis meant that, before the record could be tackled, Matt had to put in a lot of work to remind himself of the skills that he needed.

For their record attempt, Matt and Judy would be towed into the air by Matt's instructor, Chris Dawes, flying a microlite.

It was important for Matt and Judy to rehearse everything on the ground that might happen in the air, and Chris and Judy also took Matt through a series of trial runs at low altitude. It is physically hard work flying a hang-glider, and Judy and Matt would need to work as a team to break the record. Their smiles hid a lot of nervousness!

Any world record has to be checked independently. Mark Dale was our adjudicator, and he sat on the ground with Matt's dad and Meg to check on the progress of the flight. Mark showed Matt the tiny altimeter that would measure the height of the hang-glider and confirm the record.

When Chris set off in the microlite, pulling the hang-glider on a strong line behind him, Matt and Judy knew that this was their moment. And what a moment!

"It was hard work keeping the hang-glider balanced as we climbed,"

says Matt, "but we were prepared for a bit of pain!" The existing record was 8,000 feet. To break it, they had to reach at least 8,400 feet.

"I could read my own instruments and I knew when we'd got there. It was a great moment, but there was no time to celebrate. We were both feeling good and we knew we could go higher."

Chris finally pulled the release cord at 11,000 feet. Matt and Judy were on their own, and they even rose a bit higher. It was a new world record! But they still had to pilot the hang-glider back to the ground. There is less oxygen in the air at high altitudes, so Matt and Judy were wearing masks to help them breathe. It was Matt's job to turn on the oxygen. After twenty minutes, the flight was almost over, and Matt and Judy returned to the landing strip with their "world record" smoke flare burning behind them.

"It was a fantastic feeling to know we'd smashed that record."

There's always a birthday or an anniversary looming that you need to get a present for. It could be your mum's, grandad's or big sister's. These picture boxes are ideal for everyone. You can put teddies, flowers or toy Ferraris inside them, and they can be made cheaply and easily.

Collect together these ingredients and then you can get started.

You will need:

A deep margarine tub

Wire

Sticky tape

Newspaper

PVA glue

Kitchen paper

Paint

Corrugated cardboard

Clear plastic film (from an empty food package like a cake box)

Something cute to put inside the picture box

2 Paint the box in a nice colour. Small sample pots of emulsion paint are ideal for this. If you choose a pale shade, it's worth giving it a coat of white paint first.

1 Wash and dry the margarine tub. Tape a loop of wire to the base. The picture box can be hung from this. Tear up strips of newspaper and use diluted PVA glue to stick the strips all over the outside of the tub. Allow to dry. Repeat with torn strips of kitchen paper. This gives a textured, hand-made look.

FRAME

3 To make the frame for the picture box, measure the tub and draw a rectangle I cm smaller on a piece of corrugated cardboard.

4 Draw another rectangle around the first, roughly 4cm larger. Draw freehand curves in pencil at each corner, and then cut out the frame shape.

5 As with the box, cover the frame with newspaper and kitchen paper before painting it. If you want a shiny frame, use acrylic paint.

6 Select something small and appropriate that fits in the tub and would look good hanging on the wall or resting on a shelf.

7 If you choose something like a tiny teddy bear that might move around, cut a rectangle of card and fold it in two places to form a Z. Glue one section to the bottom of the tub and glue the teddy to the top section. Make sure it is the same way up as the wire loop. Leave to dry.

8 Cut a piece of clear plastic film slightly larger than the open side of the tub and glue it to the frame.

9 When it has dried, glue the 'glazed' frame to the tub and rest a heavy book on top to ensure it sticks firmly.

And there you have it. A perfect present for someone special!

Amazing

Meg is the baby of the Blue Peter team. She'll be three in December, and just like all Border Collies, was born to be a working sheep dog.

It's a tricky business keeping Meg up to speed with everything she has learnt, but fortunately my old friend, Derek Bowmer, always comes up with a plan to help my four-legged television star do her stuff.

This time Derek organized a Young Handlers' Competition in Catterick. Competitors travelled from all over the UK, and it was to be Meg's first real sheep dog trial. The man to impress was Sandy Beaton, a well-known judge at the English National Trials and the World Championships.

Apart from my family rolling up to give us support, Meg's mum and sister were also among the spectators. No pressure then!

The competition was divided into categories according to the age of the handler. The course we were to follow was pretty standard, and, if all went to plan, Meg would be fine. Points would be scored for each of the tasks performed.

14   RHP-233   16   FUJ

14   36 ▷14A   16   36 ▷16

Meg

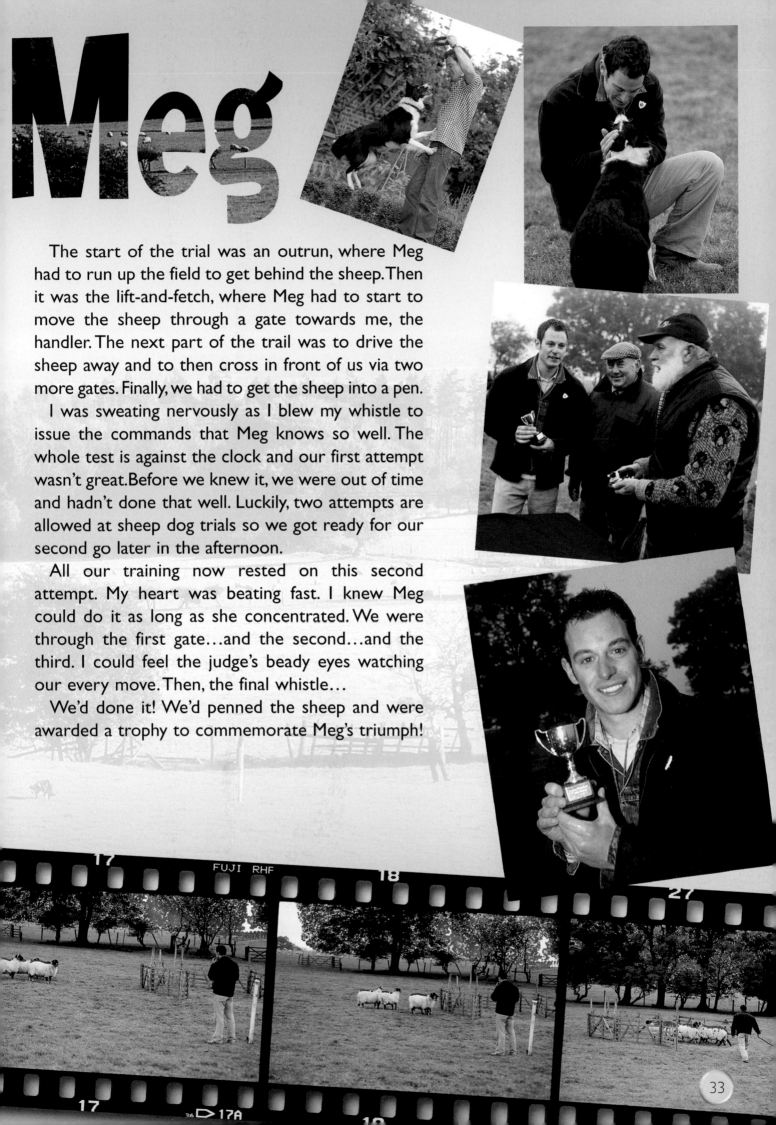

The start of the trial was an outrun, where Meg had to run up the field to get behind the sheep. Then it was the lift-and-fetch, where Meg had to start to move the sheep through a gate towards me, the handler. The next part of the trail was to drive the sheep away and to then cross in front of us via two more gates. Finally, we had to get the sheep into a pen.

I was sweating nervously as I blew my whistle to issue the commands that Meg knows so well. The whole test is against the clock and our first attempt wasn't great. Before we knew it, we were out of time and hadn't done that well. Luckily, two attempts are allowed at sheep dog trials so we got ready for our second go later in the afternoon.

All our training now rested on this second attempt. My heart was beating fast. I knew Meg could do it as long as she concentrated. We were through the first gate…and the second…and the third. I could feel the judge's beady eyes watching our every move. Then, the final whistle…

We'd done it! We'd penned the sheep and were awarded a trophy to commemorate Meg's triumph!

The castle of Neuschwanstein is just like something out of a fairy tale or a cartoon, and, in fact, was the inspiration for the castle in Disney's Magic Kingdom in Florida. It was the creation of the Dream King – Ludwig II of Bavaria, and Liz travelled to Germany in search of his strange and fascinating story.

Ludwig was born on 25 August 1845. As a boy, he spent many hours playing with toy bricks and, when he grew up, creating bizarre and extravagant buildings became the greatest passion of his life.

His childhood was strict and often lonely. Even his pet tortoise was taken away from him because it was thought he was getting too fond of it.

He became King very suddenly, aged just eighteen – and to his people he seemed like a real-life Prince Charming. He loved dressing up, and his image was always very important to him.

"If I didn't have my hair curled every day, I couldn't enjoy my food," Ludwig said!

Dream King

Now toy bricks were a thing of the past and Ludwig let his imagination run riot. Spending lavishly on his buildings, he refined and changed everything right up to the last moment.

Ludwig didn't care what it took to achieve his vision, saying, "I don't want to know how it works, I just want to see the effect!"

He was very shy and had few friends, but was fascinated by swans and peacocks. He spent so much of his life hidden away in his fabulous and often bizarre palaces that he became known as the Dream King.

Ludwig was strongly influenced by his deep friendship with the German composer, Richard Wagner.

Wagner's music was explosively dramatic, and inspired Ludwig in his ceaseless building. But few people approved of this friendship or of the money which he showered on the composer.

Liz explored two of Ludwig's most celebrated creations by walking through the golden rooms in the palace of Linderhof, and taking a helicopter flight over the castle of Neuschwanstein – a breathtaking experience.

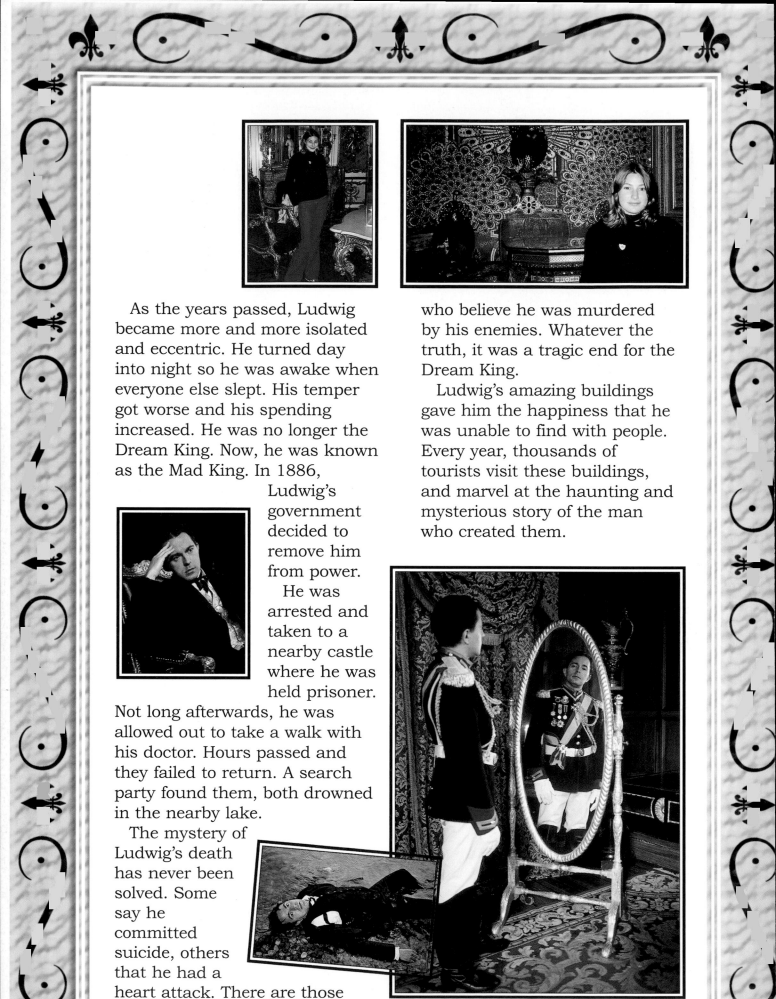

As the years passed, Ludwig became more and more isolated and eccentric. He turned day into night so he was awake when everyone else slept. His temper got worse and his spending increased. He was no longer the Dream King. Now, he was known as the Mad King. In 1886, Ludwig's government decided to remove him from power.

He was arrested and taken to a nearby castle where he was held prisoner. Not long afterwards, he was allowed out to take a walk with his doctor. Hours passed and they failed to return. A search party found them, both drowned in the nearby lake.

The mystery of Ludwig's death has never been solved. Some say he committed suicide, others that he had a heart attack. There are those who believe he was murdered by his enemies. Whatever the truth, it was a tragic end for the Dream King.

Ludwig's amazing buildings gave him the happiness that he was unable to find with people. Every year, thousands of tourists visit these buildings, and marvel at the haunting and mysterious story of the man who created them.

Gorgeous George!

In June 1982 a magnificent Mediterranean Spur Thigh tortoise made his first appearance on Blue Peter. He was christened George, and has been popping in and out of the studio and meandering around the Blue Peter garden for the last twenty-one years!

After George had been happily taking part in the programme for six years, he became the talk of the nation. When the house where he lived was burgled, and his pen in the garden was opened, George went to seek pastures new. After weeks of searching, everyone thought he was lost forever. A sad announcement was made on the show, but within forty-eight hours a viewer's Jack Russell terrier called Tod had sniffed him out in nearby woods. A grand reunion was organized in the Blue Peter garden, and everyone heaved a huge sigh of relief that George was safely back home.

Over the years, George has made friends with presenters, who have always been keen to give him a gentle bath before and after hibernation.

Imagine how astounded we were when George was examined by a herpetologist – a reptile expert – who declared him to be eighty years old!

The year 2003 marks George's twenty-first anniversary on Blue Peter, and, with a life expectancy of over a hundred years, we hope that there will be many more happy returns.

HORSES' HOLIDAY

T he Household Cavalry are famous all over the world for their splendid ceremonial displays. The horses, and the soldiers who ride and look after them, are based in a huge barracks in London. But, for a few weeks every summer, they leave the city and head for their camp in the Norfolk countryside. It's a chance for the men to brush up their riding skills and for the horses to enjoy a break from their usual routine.

I'd had a few riding lessons before I arrived, but I had no idea what my instructor, Corporal of Horse Pete Semczyszyn (known as Semtex) had planned for me. Over the next few days, I was put through my paces as I learnt the basics of show jumping, with the eventual aim of entering myself in the regimental show jumping competition.

I'd heard a lot about the bond between the horses and the men, and my horse, Winston, really seemed to be on my side as I struggled to take my basic skills up to the level required.

Out of the saddle, a huge amount of time is spent grooming the horses and looking after them. But it wasn't all hard graft.

I'll never forget riding on the beach and taking our horses into the sea for a swim. It was such a strange sensation. I very nearly fell off, but it was an experience I wouldn't have missed for the world. Then there was the afternoon I learnt to hold the reins in one hand, a sword in the other, gallop up to a watermelon on a pole and slice it in half. To my delight, I did it in one go!

After a few days of almost non-stop riding (my backside was battered and my legs took a while to work every morning) it was time to try my luck in the show jumping competition. I had to take Winston over a series of jumps, under the expert eyes of Semtex and the assembled soldiers on camp. It was incredibly nerve-racking, but I concentrated hard, encouraging Winston all the time. The course seemed to fly by.

Thanks to Winston, Semtex's expert tuition and the encouragement of the lads, I'd done it! That afternoon, I was given a special presentation in front of the regiment. It wasn't much of a holiday, but I'd had the time of my life!

Synchro Stars

We often laugh when sports are described as being "Britain's fastest- growing sport", and when talk in the Blue Peter office turned to synchronized swimming, I was all set for a chuckle. Then I heard the words, "not normally associated with men". My smile faded when I was told that synchronized swimming would be my next assignment. And, as it is possible that there are no other male synchro swimmers in the world, I would be considered the best! This didn't make me feel any better, but Liz took one look at my shocked expression and, thankfully, volunteered to join me in a try-out with the National Champions, the Rushmore Synchronized Swimming Team.

Our training began on dry land with stretching exercises, as flexibility is the key to successful synchronized swimming. The team's coach, Adele Carlson, talked us through the routine, and then it was into the pool for a game of underwater tag. The aim of the game was to teach us to hold our breath for as long as possible. Top synchro swimmers can hold theirs for up to three minutes – the average person would struggle to hold their breath for 45 seconds!

Then it was down to business. The skills we had to learn were sculling – better known as treading water. Both Liz and I were good at this part. Next was the art of egg beating. This, believe it or not, was learning to keep your body out

of the water just by using your legs. So far, so good. Then we moved to leg lifting, and this was quite a bit trickier. We'd just about got the hang of the basics when it was time to go through the routine. The idea was that the team would form a beautiful circle, and Liz would be lifted right out of the water.

We were as ready as we'd ever be and, with some trepidation, Liz and I put on nose clips and joined the National Champions for a very special performance...

They do say every picture tells a story!

We certainly enjoyed synchronized swimming, but if you happen to know a man who thinks he is the best synchro swimmer in the world, tell him not to worry, as he'll have no competition from Mr T.

The Strange Tale of

How do you know when you're really famous? When Madame Tussaud's sculptors spend several months and thousands of pounds turning you into a wax model, that's when!

But who was Madame Tussaud, and how did a French woman create such a celebrated British institution? The story begins two hundred years ago in France, with a little girl named Marie Grosholtz.

Marie's mother worked for a talented wax sculptor, and Marie would sit for hours in his studio, watching and learning all she could.

In time she was sent to the fabulous Palace of Versailles, glittering home of the kings and queens of France.

Here she taught the king's sister, Madame Elizabeth, the fashionable art of wax modelling.

She made models of all the royal family. But outside the palace, trouble was brewing. In 1789 a bloody revolution broke out.

Madame Tussaud

Marie watched her rich and royal friends being sent to the guillotine. Afterwards, she was made to create wax models from their heads.

But Marie was tough and she survived, marrying a man called Tussaud and carrying on with her wax modelling business.

Just like today, all the great names were modelled in wax, such as the famous French leader, Napoleon Bonapartc. Each model was exact in every detail.

Eventually she decided to try her luck abroad, and brought her caravan of wax models to tour Britain. They were a huge success.

People flocked from miles around to see the wax models. In the days before television and photography, it was often their only chance to see what famous people really looked like.

After closing, Madame Tussaud would work on new models, teaching her sons the tricks of her trade.

She survived many near disasters, including a shipwreck in which she nearly lost her priceless collection of figures.

Another time, a terrible riot broke out in Bristol. Madame Tussaud ordered her sons to take the waxworks out of the back of the house before the mob could destroy them.

Finally Madame Tussaud found a permanent home for her wax figures in London's Baker Street, where they have been ever since.

She died in 1850, but you can see her likeness in the museum – and people still queue up to see the exhibition, just as they did all those years ago.

THE QUEST III

Jack dropped the queen bee back in the hive and ran. But the killer bees were between him and the door. He looked desperately around the conservatory to see if anything could save him, but there were only tropical plants and a reed-filled pond. A pond! Jack ran to it, broke off a reed which he put in his mouth, and plunged into the water. While the bees swarmed above the water, Jack lay beneath breathing through the reed, and waited…

The wind whistled around Loveday as she clung onto the clock face. Her arms were tired and she didn't know how long she could hold on for. She had one invention which might be of use but it had never been tested. Loveday double-checked that she was wearing her pink skirt with the blue trim. Then, taking a deep breath, she stepped off the edge. She fell quickly, but as the wind caught her skirt it whipped up her body, sliding past her waist and her head and up past her arms. With a jerk, her fall slowed as straps at her waist stopped the skirt from flying away, and turned it into a parachute. With her petticoats and bloomers billowing beneath her and her skirt above her head, Loveday glided gently to the ground…

The boar was thundering towards Will, its long tusks aiming straight at him. Will stood still, waiting.

When it seemed as though the boar was going to run him through, he sprang.
He dived forward and, placing his hands on the beast's back, vaulted over it. Landing in a crouch, he raced away from the puzzled boar and dashed through the woods to Chase Manor. In his hand was the locket he had snatched from the beast mid-vault. He hoped the others had managed to get the pearls…

Will arrived back at the entrance hall, where they suspected they'd find the entrance to the secret lab. Loveday was putting on her skirt and Jack was squelching through the hall, soaking wet and covered in pond weed.
   "Don't ask," said Jack.
   "So, we've got the pearls," said Will. "Now what do we do with them?"
   "Pearls before swine may become the pearls of wisdom…" murmured Loveday.
   "Which one of these objects do the pearls fit in?" wondered Jack.
   "Elementary, my dear Jack," said Loveday.
   "You really do need to get your own catchphrase," Jack replied.

Loveday knows which object in the entrance hall opens Professor Chases's laboratory. Have YOU solved the riddle? If so, turn to page 62 and find out how to enter the competition to win the Pearls of Wisdom.

Solomon
Islands

Australia

THE HAPPY

"I've travelled a lot on Blue Peter," says Simon, "but I've never been anywhere as remote as the Solomon Islands."

In fact, few television programmes have ever been filmed in these four hundred or so islands in the Pacific Ocean, but Blue Peter film producer Alex Leger had worked there before he joined the show. With an old friend, Bishop Willy Pwaisiho, he arranged for Simon to make the journey there.

"Willy is a parish priest in Macclesfield, as well as being a village leader in the Solomons," Simon explained .

With Willy, Simon explored life in the islands. "I'll never forget the greetings that we received. In one village, we were ambushed by a group of warriors. I had no idea how to react as I'd never seen anything like it in my life. But Willy told me to stay calm as it was a traditional challenge, and in the end we couldn't have been made more welcome.
The same thing happened with war canoes.
To be honest, the greeting was for Willy and not for me!"

ISLANDS

Simon travelled in the company of the Melanesian Brotherhood, a Christian group who do respected work in the islands. On their travels they visited Walande, an artificial island built centuries ago by people who had no rights to land on the main islands. The inhabitants regularly have to repair the island walls because of the high tides that flood their village. The flooding, possibly caused by global warming, is threatening their whole way of life.

"It was strange to think that problems in my world could be affecting theirs so dramatically," says Simon.

Their final destination was Willy's home village, Kolona.

"The welcome was extraordinary. The feast was massive. I helped with one of the puddings, which was much larger than the food we prepare in the studio! I was really struck by the warmth of the welcome that we received. Many of the people we met had few of the things that we consider necessary to be happy in the West, yet people like the Melanasian Brothers seemed truly happy to me. It made me think about the true meaning of happiness and what you really need in life. Possessions don't matter much if you have good people around you and a real faith. It really was a journey of a lifetime."

CHRISTMAS AT THE CLUB BLUE PETER

It was a cold, dark winter a long time ago, the perfect setting for our Christmas musical extravaganza. But wait, the best person to take you through the story is surely its hero, JJ Vanderfella the Third.

"Hi, I'm JJ. That's short for Jesse Josiah, in case you're wondering. This was taken on a night I'll never forget, my first visit to the Club Blue Peter. My new pal, Toothpick, described me as 'all muscles and money'. Well, I guess my pop did own the place! Anyhow, little did I know what was round the corner..."

"All my life I'd been full of dreams of showbiz and showgirls, and the Club Blue Peter had plenty of both. It was the hottest spot in town."

"The star was Venus Chartreuse. But Venus was a sham. She couldn't actually sing a note!"

"Club manager Big Daddy, had tricked a poor wannabe chorus girl called Minnie into signing a fifty-year contract to be Venus's voice, singing into a mike offstage while Venus mimed and got all the glory."

"Big Daddy was a real crook. Together with Venus's ghastly mother, Enchilada, they hatched a plan. Venus would pretend to love me, and in return, they reckoned I'd put up the cash for their Christmas spectacular. But, as Big Daddy's nephew (and Minnie's best friend), Junior, discovered, the greedy club manager was planning to double-cross everyone and run off with all the takings."

"Just as they predicted, I fell head over heels in love with Venus. But when I told her that I'd turned my back on my fortune to make my own way in the world, I ended up dumped in a gutter."

"Luckily, I was rescued by Minnie and Junior. With their help, I decided it was high time someone brought Venus and Big Daddy to justice. Dressed up as a waitress, I landed a job in the club, and got all the evidence I needed to tell my pop exactly what was going on."

"Big Daddy and Venus managed to escape before they could be arrested, but they were never seen in this town again.
Now I found true love with Minnie, just in time for Christmas.
And with the club under my management, Minnie became its star and Junior its leading man. A happy ending all round!"

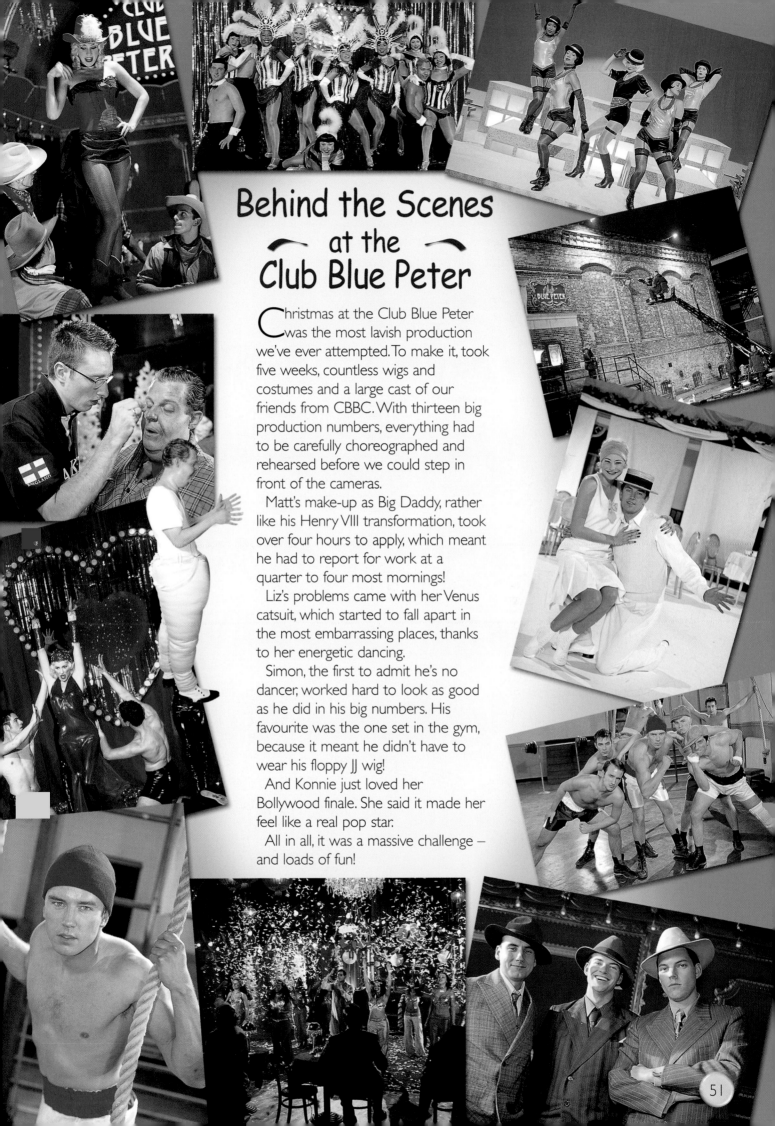

Behind the Scenes at the Club Blue Peter

Christmas at the Club Blue Peter was the most lavish production we've ever attempted. To make it, took five weeks, countless wigs and costumes and a large cast of our friends from CBBC. With thirteen big production numbers, everything had to be carefully choreographed and rehearsed before we could step in front of the cameras.

Matt's make-up as Big Daddy, rather like his Henry VIII transformation, took over four hours to apply, which meant he had to report for work at a quarter to four most mornings!

Liz's problems came with her Venus catsuit, which started to fall apart in the most embarrassing places, thanks to her energetic dancing.

Simon, the first to admit he's no dancer, worked hard to look as good as he did in his big numbers. His favourite was the one set in the gym, because it meant he didn't have to wear his floppy JJ wig!

And Konnie just loved her Bollywood finale. She said it made her feel like a real pop star.

All in all, it was a massive challenge – and loads of fun!

THE

Nobody is quite sure how New York got its nickname, the Big Apple. Some say it was coined by a bunch of musicians, others that it was dreamt up by gangsters. Whatever the truth, it stuck, and there's no doubt that the Big Apple is one of the world's most exciting cities – the city that never sleeps.

It is famous for its skyscrapers. The city's architects reasoned that, with only a small amount of land and millions of people to house, they'd have to build upwards. The most famous skyscraper was, and still is, the Empire State Building. The views from the top took our breath away. And the Statue of Liberty, which used to be the first great landmark for new arrivals to the city, was very impressive. Since the terrible events of 11 September 2001, you can no longer climb to the top.

There was a lot to cram in besides sightseeing. Matt learnt to tap dance on a rooftop studio, while I did a little

BIG APPLE

of what I love best – shopping. But not for myself! I went to one of the top stores to become a 'personal shopper' for people who are either not interested in shopping or are too busy. It's harder than it sounds because you have to think about their needs, tastes and budget, not your own.

One of our biggest challenges was the chance to join the world famous Harlem Gospel Choir on stage during one of their fantastic shows. Their joyful enthusiasm soon made us forget our nerves, and we had great fun belting out *Oh Happy Day*, though I'm not sure we lived up to our introduction as "a blue-eyed soul brother and sister"!

Keeping law and order in this teeming place is the job of the New York Police Department, or NYPD. Matt was invited to spend a day training with some of the new recruits. As well as a pounding in the gym and a timed assault course – which he passed with flying colours – he learnt how to handcuff someone correctly. Fortunately, he hasn't needed this skill since.

The hardest thing about our trip was leaving. We'd loved every minute of our time in the city that never sleeps.

Although I still get nervous from time to time, I've got used to presenting Blue Peter. But when I was told I was going to be the first presenter ever to direct a live programme, the butterflies were back big time!

09.15 Producer Mel Smith showed me the running order. This lists everything in each show – how long the items are, whether they're live or pre-recorded and who is involved. On the day, I was going to be in charge of a team of around fifty people, from cameras, sound and lighting to designers, floor managers, presenters and pets!

SIMON AS A

2.00 A planning meeting is held for the director to talk through the show and answer technical queries. "Do you want to use a boom for that?" "Will that be local VT?" "What colour do you want the floor?" The questions flew thick and fast! I tried to answer all of them, though there was a bit of bluffing!

DAY TWO

09.45 On the day, camera rehearsals started at 09.45. The crew 'blocked' through my script, listening as I gave instructions over their 'talkbacks' – radio headsets.

5.35 He seemed fairly pleased. "Could we see more of the pets, please?" was his main criticism!

16.45 I passed on Richard's changes to the crew while he briefed the presenters.

10.00 Our set is a kit of parts. Each piece is moveable and it's the director's job to decide which bits to use. Once I'd set out my model studio, I used coins to stand in for the five studio cameras.

11.00 Every programme is scripted, and I had to match the words with the right pictures. The director decides when to see a close-up of something, when to be wide – showing action or performances, how long to hold each shot, and whether the cameras should be moving or not. It needs to be planned so the camera crew know exactly what they're doing, and when.

STUDIO DIRECTOR

14.00 The director sits in the production gallery. A bank of monitors shows the output of each camera. The one in the middle shows what the viewers will see. The director is helped by the vision mixer who cuts up each shot, and the production assistant who makes sure everything runs to time.

15.30 There was a full dress rehearsal or 'run through' of the programme. It's the only chance to try the show in order, and it is watched by the series producer, Richard, who takes notes on everything from the shots to the presenters' performance.

16.55 Now there were only minutes till live transmission. The production assistant began the count, "Five, four, three, two, one…" I gave the order to run the tape of the opening titles and Blue Peter number 3578 was 'on the air'.

17.00 The next twenty-four and a half minutes flew by. Before I knew it, it was all over. I'd kept my nerve and I'd kept talking. And what's more, I'd really enjoyed being in charge!

Laurie Duncan
Age 15

dress with
aped back.

THERES NO
LIKE SHOW

...especially when it comes to choosing costumes!

When plans were underway for our Christmas extravaganza, we thought it was high time we invited our talented audience to help design some fabulous frocks for the leading lady, Miss Elizabeth Barker.

Liz was going to play the part of Venus, star attraction at the Club Blue Peter. For one of the scenes, Liz's character needed a divine dress – something spectacular that she could sing and dance in.

20,986 of you put your all into the challenge, and we had a great time looking at the sumptuous outfits you designed.

The final choice was down to Liz, but could she make up her mind? No! She was thrilled by your efforts and, in addition to the two designs to be

Ella Wheeler
Age 5

Venus Chartreuse

Tessa Lyons
Age 14

Carys Williams
Age 15

Arron Thind
Age 9

BUSINESS BUSINESS

bowling hat.

turned into costumes for the show, she picked one hundred top also-rans and another one hundred runners-up.

Liz is wearing a design by fifteen-year-old Laurie Duncan from Finchampstead on the page opposite and also on the cover. The lady loves red! She's also shown on this page in the other prize-winning costume designed by twelve-year-old Robert Hawcutt from Skegness.

Judging by the fantastic ideas sent in for this competition, we think Blue Peter viewers of today are definitely the Stella McCartneys and Alexander McQueens of the future!

P.S. If you were inspired by this competition, we think it's only a matter of time before you're discovered by one of the big fashion houses. Let us know if your work makes it to the international catwalk!

garter.

Izzy Marshall
Age 7

Joanna Barnett
Age 7

Jade Caldicott
Age 9

Amelia Rees
Age 6

Kerry Gwatkin
Age 6

Sukhdeep Digpal
Age 15

Kirsty O'Connor
Age 9

READY TO

"Arch, reach, recover…arch, reach, pull."

From his training to his first solo freefall jump, Simon had a lot to learn and very little time in which to learn it.

"My first parachute jump was from a static line in Oxfordshire, but I travelled to San Diego in California for my greatest challenge, my first-ever skydive."

Simon's first jump was attached to another parachutist – a tandem free fall. Then it was back to the ground to rehearse the routines that he would use in the air.

"My first solo jump would be accelerated free fall. I'd have Roger and Toby hanging onto me to stop me tumbling out of control. There was a lot to remember. In the end I could do it in my sleep. Before you jump, the sound of the aeroplane multiplies your nerves. The higher we climbed, the more anxious I felt. I just had to relax and not think about the wind rushing past my

body at 120mph. It all happened so quickly, I hardly had time to be frightened. When the parachute opened I was lost for words, which can't anyway begin to describe what it was like."

Simon's landing was perfect, but over the next few jumps his nerves got worse and worse.

"Only those who've known real fear will understand what I was going through."

Eventually Simon took the brave decision to stop jumping.

SKYDIVE?

"I needed a break to get my confidence back."

And sure enough, on his return to the UK, he was soon jumping again.

"I don't know how much I'll achieve in the long run, but I'm not giving up yet!"

When scouts talk about B-P, they're not referring to Blue Peter but to Baden-Powell, the founder of the entire movement. BP also stands for "Be Prepared!", the famous scouting motto.

Today there are half a million scouts in Britain, and when they say, "Be prepared!" they obviously mean it. From 2003, scouts plan to hold one hundred events a year until 2007, the centenary of the organisation. One thing is certain – Baden-Powell would have approved!

Robert Baden-Powell was born in 1857 and, as a boy, hated being stuck inside a stuffy classroom. He much preferred sailing, hiking and camping with his brothers. When he grew up, he joined the army. There he developed ideas on scouting, which he taught to young soldiers in his regiment, and wrote about in a book called *Aids to Scouting*.

In 1907 he held an experimental camp for twenty boys from very different backgrounds at Brownsea Island, Dorset. The camp was a great success, and proved to Baden-Powell that his training and methods really worked.

Next he wrote *Scouting For Boys*, issued in six fortnightly parts at four pence each. It was an immediate success. Boys everywhere were keen to try out his ideas and soon scout troops were being formed all over the world.

Baden-Powell became the first Chief Scout, and just before his death in 1941 he said, "I have had a most happy life and I want each one of you to have as happy a life, too!"

Over the years, millions of people have enjoyed being scouts. Simon was one, as were David Beckham, Chris Tarrant... The list is endless!

The image of scouting has changed since it began and so has the uniform.

This was the first version. It may look primitive now, but back then boys found it a huge improvement on the itchy, uncomfortable clothes they were used to.

This next look became popular after the First World War. All scouts had whistles, scarves (or "neckers") and, of course, as many badges as they could earn!

By the 1950s the old stetson hats were replaced with berets.

In the 1970s it was all change. No more bare knees as shorts were axed and the new uniforms were made of man-made fibres, making life easier at camp.

The latest version shown here, is smart, comfortable and colourful, and works equally well for girls, who are now just as much a part of scouting as boys!

Fitness

Outdoor Plus

Adventure

Expedition

Community

Global

61

Our address is:
Blue Peter, BBC TV Centre London,
London W12 7RJ

Our home page is:
http://www.bbc.co.uk/cbbc
e mail: bluepeter@bbc.co.uk

Written by Anne Dixon, Steve Hocking
and Richard Marson

EastEnders Market Stall and In the Frame
by Gillian Shearing
The Strange Tale of Madame Tussaud
illustrated by Bob Broomfield
Photograph of Madame Tussaud courtesy
of The Tussauds Group
Photograph of Baden Powell
and Scout Association logo courtesy
of the Scout Association
Photograph of Sven Goran Eriksson courtesy
of Richard Bryant/ Salvation Army

Photography by
Jennie Blunden, Charlie Booker, Chris
Capstick, Emma Clark, Catherine Gildea,
Martyn Goddard, John Green, Alex Leger, Kez
Margrie, Richard Marson, Simon Thomas,
and Steve Vickerstaff.

If we have left anyone out, we are sorry.

The authors would like to thank the whole
Blue Peter team for their help and ideas.
Every effort has been made to contact
copyright holders for permission to
reproduce material in this book. If any
material has been included without
permission please contact us.

First published in 2003 by
BBC Worldwide Limited
Woodlands, 80 Wood Lane,
London W12 0TT

Design and editorial by
The Dirty Cat Company/Sally FK
© BBC Worldwide Limited 2003
Blue Peter word logo © BBC 1985
Blue Peter ship logo © BBC 1963
CBBC & logo ™ BBC. © BBC 2002
ISBN 0 563 49107 8
Printed and bound in Singapore.

CAPTIONS FOR PAGES 2 AND 3

1 Simon got a taste of the super-rough, super-fast game of Aussie Rules – now being played in the UK, too.

2 Diving belle Konnie Huq about to explore the ocean off Hawaii.

3 What a prize! Simon with Blue Peter competition winner, Eve Woodrow, whose football team's prize was a training session from England manager Sven Goran Eriksson.

4 Matt travelled to Austria to master the highs – and lows – of snowboarding.

5 Liz in the pilot's seat with the crew of the world's fastest passenger plane, the supersonic Concorde.

6 Bizarre cars on Blue Peter – Konnie loved her spin in a replica Wacky races roadster.

7 Launching our Blue Peter Dog's Alphabet with A for Alaskan Malamutes.

8 The RAF Queen's Squadron surprised us with an impressive display of marching to the sound of Kylie Minogue!

9 Konnie and Liz let it rip, roaring around a racing circuit – on lawnmowers!

10 Liz as practically perfect Princess Banana and Simon as Dr Sam Bennett battling the evil Gul in the Quest.

11 Our studio was filled with the colour and noise of the Russian Cossack dancers.

12 Simon giving his all during the 60 metre sprint in the Indoor Athletic Championships in Manchester.

13 Baker meets Bond. Face to face with the movie legend, Pierce Brosnan, on the set of the latest James Bond movie.

14 They say a mountie always gets his man. Not sure about these two likely lads, though!

15 Gareth Gates backed the winners of our Blue Peter dancing competition.

THE QUEST

You could win the Pearls of Wisdom and collect them in person from the Blue Peter studio if you can tell us which object in the entrance hall was used by the detectives to open Professor Chase's top-secret laboratory. Cut out and fill in the entry slip, and send it to: Blue Peter Quest, PO Box 20, London W12 6BP The closing date is 28th February 2004.

Name...Age.............

Address...

....

The object is..